LET'S LOOK AT...

Birds

OF THE
BRITISH ISLES

Lucy Beevor

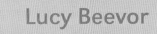

Raintree is an imprint of Capstone Global Library Limited, a company incorporated in England and Wales having its registered office at 264 Banbury Road, Oxford, OX2 7DY – Registered company number: 6695582

www.raintree.co.uk
myorders@raintree.co.uk
Text © Capstone Global Library Limited 2019
The moral rights of the proprietor have been asserted.

Edited by Clare Lewis
Designed by Cynthia Della-Rovere
Original illustrations © Capstone Global Library Limited 2018
Picture research by Tracy Cummins
Production by Tori Abraham
Originated by Capstone Global Library Ltd
Printed and bound in India

ISBN 978 1 4747 6389 9 (hardback)
22 21 20 19 18
10 9 8 7 6 5 4 3 2 1

ISBN 978 1 4747 6393 6 (paperback)
23 22 21 20 19
10 9 8 7 6 5 4 3 2 1

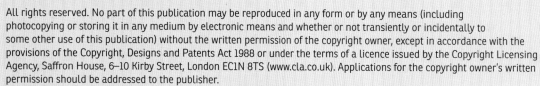
British Library Cataloguing in Publication Data
A full catalogue record for this book is available from the British Library.

Acknowledgements
We would like to thank the following for permission to reproduce photographs: We would like to thank the following for permission to reproduce photographs: Alamy: BIOSPHOTO/Frederic Desmette, 11 Bottom, blickwinkel/Hecker, 21 Top, Glyn Thomas, 28 BL, jack perks, 20 TR, Jordon Sharp, 16 Top, PAUL R. STERRY, 15 BL, 15 MB, Scubazoo, 17 Top; Dreamstime: Tramper2, 9 TR; Getty Images: Arterra/UIG, 12 MR; Minden Pictures: Denis Bringard, 21 MB, Jane Burton, 21 BL, Jelger Herder, 21 BR; Shutterstock: Alexander Raths, 29 BL, Andrew Balcombe, 11 Middle, Andrew Roland, 6 Middle, Ant Cooper, 26 Top, aquapix, 5 TM, Bright, 10 Bottom, chris froome, 9 TL, Chris Moody, 7 MR, Christian Schoissingeyer, 2, 12 BL, Coatesy, 8 Right, colin robert varndell, 5 BR, Dirk Ercken, 20 BR, DJTaylor, 5 BL, Eddie J. Rodriquez, 4 Top, Erni, 16 BR, Ervin Monn, 7 TR, ESK Imagery, 24 BL, Gail Johnson, 13 Middle, Grant M Henderson, 24 TR, Heiko Kiera, 12 TR, Helen Hotson, 5 TL, 7 TL, Henrik Larsson, 27 TR, Hugh Lansdown, 28 TL, irin-k, 27 BL, Jakinnboaz, 19 Bottom, James Pearce, 5 MB, JASON STEEL, 7 BL, Jiri Prochazka, 16 BL, Karel Gallas, 27 BR, Kletr, Cover TL, 22 BL, lanaid12, 25 BR, Lisa S., 29 BR, Lynsey Allan, 25 Left, Maciej Olszewski, 26 Middle, Mantonature, 19 Top, Marco Maggesi, 18 Top, Mark Bridger, 22 Top, Mark Medcalf, 9 BL, Martin Fowler, 19 Middle, 28 TR, MF Photo, 14, Michal Ninger, 1, 7 ML, Migel, 24 BR, Mirko Graulo, Cover Bottom, Miroslav Hlavko, Cover Back, 10 TR, MP cz, 24 TL, N Mrtgh, 27 TL, nnnnae, Design Element, Patila, 29 Middle, Peter Turner Photography, 17 Bottom, Peter Wey, 32, Philip Bird LRPS CPAGB, 6 Bottom, Podolnaya Elena, 23 BR, Redai Paul Stefan, 15 BR, Richard Bowden, 11 Top, Rostislav Stefanek, 23 BL, 23 TR, Rudmer Zwerver, 3, 8 Left, 9 BR, 10 TL, 13 Top, 29 TR, Sakurra, 22 BR, Sandra Standbridge, Cover TR, 5 TR, snapgalleria, 28 BR, Stephan Morris, 12 BR, Sue Berry, 6 Top, Susana_Martins, 25 MR, taviphoto, Cover Middle, Tory Kallman, 13 Bottom, Uve Kirsch, 26 Bottom, Valentina Moraru, 15 TR, 18 Bottom, Vicky Jirayu, 7 BR, Vladimir Wrangel, 23 TL, 25 TR, WitR, 20 Left, Wolfgang Simlinger, 15 TL.

Contents

Some words are shown in bold, **like this**. You can find out what they mean by looking in the glossary.

LET'S LOOK AT
British birds!

Britain is famous for its bird life. There are so many places to spot birds of all types, from beaches to busy cities. Read on to find out more about these **habitats** and meet some of the birds that live there!

GARDENS

Birds are easy to spot in gardens. Some people leave out food for birds, such as long-tailed tits, especially in the winter. Birds are useful to gardeners as they eat garden pests, such as caterpillars and slugs.

long-tailed tit

4

ON THE COAST

The sea cliffs around Britain are busy with bird life! Big groups of sea birds, like the guillemot, nest on steep sea cliffs. Other birds can be seen on beaches and on **sand dunes**.

guillemots

LAKES AND RIVERS

Many types of bird live near rivers, lakes and canals. Some search the water for frogs, toads and fish to eat. Egrets build their nests in bushes on riverbanks.

egret

What is a habitat?

A habitat is the area where an animal or plant lives. Birds live in the habitat that best suits them. Many small birds, such as house sparrows, stay in parks and gardens. They hide from **predators** in trees and **shrubs**.

sparrow

TOWNS AND CITIES

Some wild birds live among us in towns and cities. They nest in trees in parks and often find food in rubbish bins and gardens. Seagulls can be seen flying high over buildings, on the lookout for food. Birds of prey, such as falcons, can even be found nesting on tall skyscrapers!

falcon

capercaillie

WOODLANDS

Woodlands are large areas of land covered with tall trees. Lots of different birds live in woodland. The capercaillie is a rare bird. It searches the forest floor for berries, nuts and seeds to eat.

GRASSLANDS AND HEATHLANDS

These are wide open spaces covered in grass, low plants and **shrubs**. Many birds, such as partridges and grouse, live near grasslands. They can easily find food on this open ground.

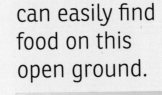

partridge

Bird body parts

Bristle feathers
Bristle feathers are strong, like the bristles on a brush. They protect the bird's eyes, nose and mouth.

Beak
All birds have bills, or beaks. They use them for eating, feeding young and preening their feathers.

Contour feathers
Contour feathers cover a bird's body. They are often colourful. They are important for flying.

Wings
All birds have wings. Most birds use their wings for flying.

Oil gland
The oil gland is a body part near a bird's tail. It holds a special oil. The bird collects the oil with its bill. It spreads the oil over its feathers to make them waterproof.

Skeleton
Birds have very light bones. This makes them light enough to fly. But their bones are also strong. Strong bones are good for takeoff and landing.

Breast
The breast is the front part of a bird's body. It is usually a different colour from the flank.

Flank
The flank is the side part of a bird's body.

Down feathers
Down feathers are small, soft and fluffy. They keep the bird warm.

Feet
A bird's feet are covered in hard scales. Most birds have sharp claws and a hallux (back toe). They are good for gripping tree branches and grabbing food.

Garden birds

It can be fun to spot garden birds from the comfort of your own home. Many birds visit gardens to find food or to nest in **shrubs** and bushes. You can attract birds by leaving out nuts or seeds for them. You can even hang up a nesting box. You might get baby birds in your garden!

ROBIN

Adult robins are easily recognizable by their bright red breasts. Robins often stay near the same garden for a long time, especially if food is left for them. They sing all year round.

BLACKBIRD

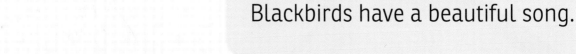

Blackbirds are one of the most common birds in the UK. Females are brown. Males are black with bright orange beaks. Blackbirds have a beautiful song.

HOUSE SPARROW

Sparrows love to eat little scraps of food. They can often be found living near humans, in garden and towns. They guard their areas **aggressively** – even tearing apart other birds' nests!

TITS

There are many types of tits in the UK. The great tit is the largest. It is green and yellow with a black head. In the winter, tits often travel in flocks to look for food in gardens and in the countryside. Blue tits usually live very near to where they hatch. So, if you spot one in your garden you will probably see it again.

blue tit

great tit

DUNNOCK

Dunnocks are a common sight in gardens. They usually feed on the ground, staying close to hedges and fences for safety.

SONG THRUSH

Song thrushes have brown feathers and speckled breasts. They like to eat snails. The birds break into them by smashing them against stones.

WREN

The wren is a tiny brown bird with a round body. Even though it is small it has a very loud singing voice!

FINCHES

chaffinch

Finches are small birds with forked tails. Some have brightly-coloured feathers. There are many types of finches. Chaffinches have long, slim beaks. They are able to pull out seeds from prickly thistles that other birds cannot reach. Goldfinches have bright red faces and yellow patches on their wings.

goldfinch

MAGPIE

Magpies are larger than most other birds you might see in the garden. They are also very noisy, with a chattering call. Magpies store food if they find a good supply. They make a small hole in the ground with their beak, drop the food in and then cover it with grass or leaves.

DOVE

Collared doves are common all around the UK. However, they can often be seen in gardens, looking for food. They eat seeds, grains and the young shoots of plants.

STARLING

Starlings are noisy birds that are often seen in large flocks. They gather in the evening to fly and swoop in large numbers. This is called a murmuration. Then they settle down to roost in trees.

On the coast

The coast is an important **habitat** for many birds. The sea can be rough and stormy, but it is home to the fish and other sea creatures that these birds eat. Rocky cliffs provide safe places for nests. **Wading** birds paddle in shallow water on **mudflats** and beaches. They look for shellfish and snails to feed on.

GANNET

Gannets are our largest seabirds. They dive down into the sea like arrows to catch fish. They can hit the water at 100 kilometres per hour!

OYSTERCATCHER

Oystercatchers wade in the shallow water on their long, pink legs. They look for shellfish, such as cockles and mussels to eat.

CORMORANT

Cormorants feed by diving to catch fish. They can dive as deep as 45 metres. Their **webbed** feet help them to swim underwater. They use their wings to steer.

PUFFIN

Puffins spend most of their lives at sea. They only come to land to nest. Their beaks turn from a dull grey to bright orange in the spring. Puffins are excellent swimmers. They dive deep underwater, looking for fish to eat. They are fantastic flyers too.

HERRING GULL

There are many types of gulls in the UK. Herring gulls are large and noisy. They live on coasts but can also be seen around rubbish tips and in towns and cities. They eat all sorts of things – even small mammals and young birds.

KITTIWAKE

Kittiwakes get their name from the call they make – "kittee-wa-wake!" They are a type of gull. Unlike other gulls, they nest high up on cliffs. The chicks stay very still so they don't fall from the nests.

ARCTIC TERN

These small gulls make some of the longest journeys of any bird in the world. Many nest in Scotland and Ireland. From there, they can fly as far south as Australia or South Africa.

Migration

Not all birds live in Britain all year round. Some visit our shores in spring to mate. Others fly from Britain to warmer countries in winter to find food. This is called migration.

Birds that **migrate** follow the same path year after year. But how do they know where to go? They use the sun, moon and stars to tell them where to fly! They also follow rivers, roads and valleys. Some birds, such as pigeons, have a special part in their brain, a bit like a **compass**. It tells them what direction to fly in.

Many birds have very long journeys. In spring, the manx shearwater flies from South America to Britain to mate. This journey is over 10,000 kilometres!

manx shearwater

Freshwater birds

Ponds, lakes, rivers and wetlands make wonderful **habitats** for many birds. Freshwater birds are often excellent divers and swimmers. They have thick feathers to keep them warm and waterproof.

GOOSE

Geese are well-known for flying together in a "V" shape. Some geese **migrate** to other countries in the winter, so they can fly a long way in that shape. Geese live near lakes and rivers. Their nests are flat and wide, and are made from grass, twigs, mud and feathers.

DUCK

There are several types of ducks that live in Britain. They have **webbed** feet for swimming and waterproof feathers. You can often see mating pairs of males and females together in spring.

SWAN

Swans are the largest members of the duck and goose family. They can often be seen gliding across lakes and ponds. Swans can sleep on water or on land. A male swan is called a cob. A female is called a pen. Their babies are called cygnets.

Do male and female birds look the same?

Male and female birds often look very different. Most male birds, such as mallards, have bold, brightly coloured feathers. This helps the male to attract a female mate. Female mallards have dull, dark feathers. This helps the mother to blend into the background as she protects the nest.

HERON

These birds have long necks and long legs for **wading** through water. They wait quietly and without moving by the sides of rivers and streams. Then they pounce, using their sharp bills to catch fish.

MooRHen

Moorhens can be spotted by their black feathers and red beaks. They often build their nests among plants or reeds on ponds or lakes. The babies that hatch can swim well. They are like little black balls of fluff!

KingFisHer

Kingfishers perch in trees or on posts and watch for fish in rivers and streams. When they spot one, they work out how deep it is by bobbing their head up and down. They dive into the water to catch their fish dinner. As they dive, see-through eyelids protect their eyes.

Woodland birds

Woodlands make good homes for many types of birds. They are full of insects and seeds that birds like to eat. Trees, **shrubs** and sheltered ground make good places for building nests. Sometimes it can be hard to spot birds in woods. But if you listen, you will hear them singing and calling.

CHIFFCHAFF

Chiffchaffs are named after the noise they make when they sing. They are small and greeny-brown coloured. They grab insects in trees to eat, or sometimes catch them in mid-air.

WILLOW WARBLER

Willow warblers look similar to chiffchaffs. But they have a very different song. Their song is more like a whistle of many notes. Willow warblers make nests close to the ground, in grass or shrubs. The nest is like a little oven. Willow warbler eggs are tiny.

CUCKOO

Cuckoos fly to Britain from Africa. They arrive here in spring. But they only stay for a few weeks. This is because cuckoos lay their eggs in other birds' nests. They do not need to stay to raise their young. The other birds do the job for them!

NIGHTINGALE

It is rare to see a nightingale. They are small and shy, and hide in thick bushes. They are known for the male's beautiful song that can sometimes be heard at night. Nightingales are able to make over 1,000 different sounds!

Why do birds sing?

When birds sing, they are actually "talking" to other birds. Songbirds, such as finches, sing long, pretty tunes. Some male birds sing to guard their **territory**. They perch on a branch and sing out loud! This warns other males to stay away. Some male birds sing to tell females that they are ready to mate. Females choose the best singers. Many songbirds sing together as the sun rises. This is called the **dawn chorus**.

A bird call is a loud peep, squawk or chatter. These are all types of warning sounds. Birds usually make these sounds when a **predator** is nearby.

blackcap
warbler

WOODPECKER

Woodpeckers spend a lot of time clinging to trees. Their strong, sharp beaks are good for pecking holes in tree trunks. They tap the bark to get at insects inside. They also eat the tasty tree **sap**.

NUTHATCH

Nuthatches look like a small woodpecker. They cannot make holes in wood, like woodpeckers can. But they use their beaks to remove bits of bark. They eat the minibeasts that they find underneath. The nuthatch is the only bird in the UK that can run down tree trunks! They happily sit upside down, clinging to the tree.

CARRION CROW

Carrion crows **adapt** easily to different **habitats**. They can be found in towns and parks, as well as in woodland. Sometimes they hide food to save it for later. They also make a clear "caw-caw" sound.

JAY

Jays are related to crows. They are much more colourful, though. They are shy birds but can sometimes be spotted flying between trees in forests.

How do birds grow?

EGG: After birds have built a nest, the female bird lays her eggs. She sits on the eggs to keep them warm. This makes the baby bird grow properly inside the egg.

HATCHLING: A hatchling is a baby bird that has just hatched out of its egg. Its feathers haven't grown yet. Its eyes are covered by thin skin. Hatchlings have a special egg tooth. They use it to break open the egg. It drops off a few days later.

CHICK: Chicks are baby birds. They have grown their first fluffy feathers. They can now use their eyes.

FLEDGLING: Fledglings are birds that are ready to take their first flight. They are getting bigger and stronger. They have grown flight feathers.

JUVENILE: A juvenile is a young bird. It is around five or six weeks old. It has grown all of its flight feathers and has strong wing muscles. It is now ready to leave the nest.

ADULT: When a bird is fully grown it is an adult. Adult birds start to look for a mate. Then the female will lay its own eggs.

hatchling

fledgling

adult

Grasslands

Some birds live best in grasslands and **heathlands**. Long grass and thickly growing plants, such as heather and gorse, make good places for nesting. Heathlands are important **habitats** for insects, and the birds and animals that eat them. Many areas have been turned into farmland or forests in the past. Now many heathlands and grasslands are **protected** by law. This is good news for the birds that live there.

QUAIL

Quails are smaller game birds. They are the only game birds in the UK that **migrate** in the winter (see page 13). They fly as far away as Africa.

PHEASANT

Game birds are birds that some people hunt for food. Pheasants, partridges, grouse and quails are all game birds. Pheasants are easy to spot in the countryside or even in gardens. Males have a red and green head. They have long tails. Pheasants can fly for a short time but they usually prefer to run.

PARTRIDGE

Partridges are plump birds. Grey partridges have distinct orange faces. Red-legged partridges have red legs and beaks. Partridges usually eat leaves, roots and seeds. Sometimes they eat insects, too.

RED GROUSE

Grouse like to live in heather. The red grouse looks a bit like a partridge. It has reddish-brown feathers. Grouse nest on the ground, in little dips that they line with grass. Both the males and females help to look after the chicks until they are ready to fly.

SKYLARK

Skylarks are famous for their beautiful, long songs. Males tell other birds to keep away by swooping up high in the sky and then back down again, singing all the way. Skylarks often nest on farmland, among grasses and crops.

NIGHTJAR

Nightjars eat insects such as moths and beetles. They hunt for them at dawn and dusk. Nightjars sleep during the day. Their brown and grey speckled feathers keep them camouflaged while they rest.

Do all birds sleep at night?

Some birds are active during the day and sleep at night. They are called **diurnal** birds. Some birds, such as most owls and nightjars, are active at night and sleep during the day. They are called **nocturnal** birds.

Towns and cities

Many birds have **adapted** to live in towns and cities. As well as the birds that visit gardens and parks, some birds prefer living near or on buildings. There is lots of food available in cities, often thrown away by humans. Tall buildings provide safe places for nesting. Birds also move to towns and cities because they have to. There are now fewer countryside **habitats** for birds. Humans are cutting down woodland and hedges to make way for more homes and roads.

PARAKEET

Parakeets are not native to the UK. Some people think the first ones escaped from captivity years ago. Now thousands of parakeets live wild in London and the surrounding area.

HOUSE MARTIN

House martins make their mud nests under the roofs of houses and other buildings. They rarely come down to the ground. Instead, they spend their time darting through the sky. They catch flying insects to eat as they go. Their forked tails help them go even faster.

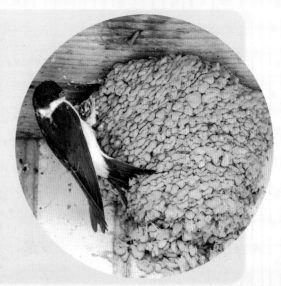

PIGEON

Pigeons are a common sight in busy cities. They build their nests high up on the window ledges of buildings. They feed on seeds, berries and insects in parks and gardens. But they are also happy to eat food dropped by humans. In cities, they can be quite tame.

GULL

Gulls usually live by the sea. If they can't find enough fish, they come to live in towns and cities. They search for food left by humans. They build nests on high buildings.

PEACOCK

Male peacocks are easy to recognize by their extremely long and beautiful tail feathers. They spread these pretty feathers when attracting a female. Peacocks are originally from India. People first brought them here to live in gardens. Now you can see them in city parks and in the grounds of stately homes.

Nests

Birds usually make nests in the spring. They lay their eggs in them. When the eggs hatch, the baby birds stay in the nest until they are old enough to leave. Different birds use different types of nests. They make them in different places.

BURROWS

Burrows are holes in the ground or in a cliff. Sand martins use their bills and feet to dig burrows in sandy cliffs. They lay their eggs in the burrow. This keeps the eggs safe from **predators** on the ground.

sand martin

EYRIES

osprey

An eyrie is a large nest high up on a mountain, hill or tree. Large birds of prey, such as osprey, nest in eyries.

CUPS

swallows

Cups are deep nests, shaped like a cup. Swallows build cup-shaped nests. They use their saliva (spit) to "glue" feathers, leaves and small twigs together.

FLOATING NESTS

Floating nests float and are surrounded by water. This protects the nest from land predators, like foxes or weasels.

great crested grebe

IN WALLS

Some small birds, like house sparrows, build their nests in any tiny hole they can find! They squeeze into holes in brick walls or under roof tiles.

house sparrow

little ringed plover

SCRAPES

Scrapes are shallow dents in the ground. The little ringed plover lays its eggs in scrapes on pebble beaches.

little owl

TREE HOLES

Owls, such as the little owl, rest in tree holes. These holes provide shelter from the rain and wind.

Birds of prey

Birds of prey are birds that hunt smaller birds and other animals to eat. These birds are built for hunting. They have excellent eyesight. They can spot **prey** from high overhead. Then they swoop down to catch it. They use large, curved **talons** to catch, grip and crush their prey. Their beaks are sharp and hooked, good for tearing apart meat. There are many birds of prey in the UK, including owls, buzzards and falcons.

BUZZARD

The buzzard is Britain's most common bird of prey. They can survive in many different **habitats**. They nest in tall trees. As well as hunting small animals and birds, they also eat earthworms!

FALCON

These birds of prey are fast flyers. They can be both big and small. The peregrine falcon is large and powerful. The merlin falcon is Britain's smallest bird of prey.

peregrine falcon

GOLDEN EAGLE

Eagles are large birds of prey. The golden eagle is one of the largest birds in Britain. It can be found in Scotland and Northern Ireland. There are very few golden eagles in the UK. They are now a **protected** species.

KESTREL

Kestrels often hover in one place watching for prey, such as voles and mice, on the ground below. When they spot something, they dive down and hold the prey against the ground in their talons.

RED KITE

Nearly 100 years ago there were only two pairs of red kites in the UK. They had been hunted and were dying out. People have worked hard to protect them and their habitats. Now you can often spot red kites soaring high above roads. They mainly eat carrion (dead animals) but can also hunt animals if they need to.

OSPREY

The osprey is an impressive bird of prey. It only eats fish. It dives into the water and uses sharp talons to grab its prey.

Owls look quite different from other birds of prey. They have large, round heads and flat faces. Most owls hunt at night. Their big eyes help them to spot **prey** in the dark. There are six types of owls in Britain. As well as those shown here, there are also the short-eared owl and Eurasian eagle owl.

BARN OWL

Barn owls have very good hearing. This helps them find prey even when it is totally dark. Their feathers are very soft. This means they can fly silently to catch their prey. Barn owls swallow their food whole. Then they cough up any fur or bones in **pellets**.

BROWN OWL

Brown owls are sometimes called tawny owls. You may be able to hear them at night. The female makes a 'to-whit' sound and the male answers with a 'woo-woo-oo' sound.

LITTLE OWL

The little owl is the UK's smallest owl. It has a short, flat head, which it nods up and down if it is frightened. The little owl can be seen in the daytime. It likes to live in open fields and farmland. It hunts for small mammals and sometimes smaller birds.

LONG-EARED OWL

This owl has long tufts of feathers that stick up on its head. The tufts look like ears but the ears are actually holes under the feathers. The long-eared owl lives in forests. It is long and thin and has dark orange eyes.

How do birds move?

We know that many birds are fantastic flyers. And water birds are often excellent swimmers. But birds can also run, hover, dive and glide.

HOVER When a bird hovers it stays in one place in the air. It needs to flap its wings quickly to stay put. Kestrels hover above fields, looking for a mouse or vole to catch.

kestrel

DIVE Diving birds, such as the grebe, plunge headfirst into water to search for food.

SOAR Many larger birds, such as red kites, soar through the sky. This means that they can fly without having to flap their wings all the time.

DASH Pied wagtails dash across the bare ground. They are searching for minibeasts, such as beetles, worms and spiders, to eat.

pied wagtail

DART Some birds, like barn swallows, dart through the air. They have long, pointed wings and forked tails. This helps them fly fast and make quick turns.

WADE When birds **wade** they walk through shallow water. Sandpipers and curlews have long legs for wading. This stops their feathers from getting wet.

curlew

CLIMB Some birds spend more time climbing trees than flying. Treecreepers get their name because they creep up tree trunks. They are searching for minibeasts hiding in the tree bark.

Glossary

aggressive forceful behaviour

compass device used by travellers that shows which direction is north

dawn chorus the singing of lots of birds early in the morning, just before dawn

game birds that are sometimes hunted by humans for food

habitat natural home of an animal or plant

heathland area of land covered in grasses, heather and gorse

migrate move from one region to another when the seasons change

mudflats stretch of muddy land left uncovered when the sea is out at the coast

pellet small mass of bones and feathers that birds of prey spit out

predator animal or bird that hunts other animals to eat

prey animal that is hunted by another animal

protected looked after and kept safe from harm

sand dune mound or small hill of sand, near the coast

sap liquid found inside a tree

shrub large plant with a woody stem, like a small tree

talon claw, especially on a bird of prey

territory place where a bird or animal lives

wade walk in shallow water

webbed having skin between the toes

Find out more

BOOKS

British Birds (Nature in Your Neighbourhood), Clare Collinson
(Franklin Watts, 2018)

My First Encyclopedia of British Wildlife, Richard McGinlay
(Armadillo Books, 2017)

WEBSITES

www.rspb.org.uk/birds-and-wildlife/bird-and-wildlife-guides/bird-identifier/
Use this brilliant bird identifier at the Royal Society for the Protection of Birds
(RSPB) website to find out what species you spotted.

**www.woodlandtrust.org.uk/visiting-woods/trees-woods-and-wildlife/
animals/birds/**
Explore many more British birds at the Woodland Trust website.

Index